P.E.E.R.S

The five step process towards achieving greatness

Joe McClain Jr.

Joe McClain Jr.

ISBN: 0-692656316
ISBN-13: 978-0692656310

P.E.E.R.S

The five step process towards achieving greatness

When we look at the term peers, we automatically think about the friends that we associate with. From the people we grow up with, to the ones we will meet later in life, you will always have peers (Unless it's just you in a cave).

From my travels around the world, through 19 countries, I have met many who have influenced my life in both a negative and a positive way. The ones who have affected me in a positive way, we still keep in contact to this day. I remember when I arrived at my first ship in the Navy back in 2003. It was the good ol' USS Nimitz. It was an aircraft carrier that at its max could hold up to 6100 people. Now, I know some of you are thinking how in the good hell can you remember all of those people. Well, I did know the majority of them, simply because I was a shipboard plumber. However, only a select few got to see and experience the real Joe McClain Jr.

Like I said, I was a shipboard plumber. People had a knack for clogging up their toilets with turds of death and I had the fortunate/unfortunate job of fixing it. It was a dirty job to have, but it kept me as a face in the crowd. Out of all 6,100 of those people, there were a group of guys that I rolled with over my three years onboard who were more than unique.

Actually, it wasn't anything that was too much unique or different about them. We all just had one thing in common. We liked girls and liked to party. They became my second family. We called ourselves crew MOTA SKILLZ. Who came up with the name, I really have no idea. It was a pretty large group of us and we all had each other's back. There was Bryan Lockett who we called Slim. He was from Cleveland, Ohio and stood 6'6. He kind of resembled Julius off of Remember The Titans and his stronghold was women. That is why he had the nickname "Slim Cutta." There was another Brian in the crew, but we called him Drew, which was a shortened version of his last name. He also stood 6'6, but he looked dead on like R&B singer Montell Jordan.

I couldn't stand going out with him. That boy used to take all of the girls. I remember us being out one time in a club called "Work Dat, Twerk Dat," in downtown San Diego. To say this was a ratchet spot was an understatement. Anywho, that night a young lady came up to me. She was fine as all get out. The only thing sexier in my eyes was a plate of gravy and biscuits.

I thought she was coming over to talk to me. However, when she came over, she had the audacity to ask me was I with the tall guy who looked like Montell Jordan. I wanted to drop kick her in her chest. Yea, that's what nights with Brian Muldrew were like. Continuing on, there was yet another Brian in the crew that we called "Sleepy." Now he looked dead on actor Laurence Fishburne and he hated when we used to call him that. If y'all don't know who Larry Fishburne is, he played in such movies as Boyz in the Hood, Hoodlum, The Matrix and Always Outnumbered.

Sleepy was from Shreveport, Louisiana and had a knack for dancing. You couldn't tell him anything when he was on the dance floor. He was Chris Brown before Chris Brown. The other one in the crew who had a knack for dancing was my man Terod Fuller. He was born and raised in Brooklyn, NY, and he looked dead on Fabolous, the famous rapper who hails from the same part of New York as him (It's funny how most of the guys I am naming resemble celebrities).

Then you had Bucky. Mr. Bass. Hmmm? What can I say about Bucky? Well, besides having two big ol' chompers that he had poking out of his mouth, he was an okay dude I'll say. I say ok because he had a knack for starting stuff, so it always put us in an awkward situation. He was still my boy though and forever will be. He was from Dallas, Texas, Oak Cliff was the area to be exact. Then there was Spoon. He was the token white boy out of the bunch. He was from somewhere in Southern Indiana (Greatest state on earth). Columbus or Frankfurt was the city I believe, but it's been so long that I may be wrong.

Torre G was from the down in the dirty Georgia parts. Willie was from San Diego. Deuce, crazy ass deuce, well he was from Rock Hill, South Carolina. He was the midget man out of the bunch standing 5'4. He was the one out of the bunch that would surprise you. The boy could out drink a fish in water and he loved his South Carolina Gamecocks. If you mentioned anything about Clemson, he would go off on you with the quickness.

Let me not forget about my main man Perryn "Nino" Brown who hailed from Savannah, Georgia. He had a heavy country accent and was just chill beyond belief. That was the crew. Those were my peers. Much like a good set of peers, they influenced me to do good things. Hell, I'll take it a step further and say great things. Sure there were times when we fell off track, but we always brought each other back up. Whether it was at work or in our down time, we kept each other going.

Currently, all of us have different lives. Some of us are married, married with kids, living overseas and we don't live the life that we used too. That simply just comes from age and growth. See in life we have a choice of who we want to be around. That is our peer group. Unfortunately, growing up in the slums of America, I saw many go down the wrong path with the wrong peers. I can't blame just the people, as our environment also had a hold on us as well, leaving a lot of us with no choice to do what we had to do to survive. We were young, dumb and thought that the world only operated through what we seen on a daily.

When you grow up in East Chicago, Indiana like me, you don't have much of a choice. You are stuck between Gary and Chicago, two cities that have been the murder capital of the United States on numerous occasions. We were right dead smack in the middle of all the gang and drug wars. The Vice Lords vs. The GD's. The Latin Kings vs. everybody. The ECPD police vs. the whole hood. That was how our life was. We had to hold our own or risk getting ate up by the streets.

Life doesn't always throw you a fastball which you can hit with ease. Most of the time, it throws curves, sinkers and sliders, making it difficult to survive where people like myself are from. Currently at age 31, I now look back at a lot of the peers that I used to hang around. Unfortunately, a lot of them have acquired residence in the cemetery, becoming permanent tenants well before their time.

I can go home to this day and see people I came up with strung out on drugs, destroyed by alcohol or filling up the grocery cart because they have multiple kids by multiple people. The only real jobs where I'm from are the steel mill and riverboats, which aren't a lock or guarantee. It truly is a sad sight to see.

That's why I named this book P.E.E.R.S. Our peers influence us no matter what you may think. Yes, at the end of the day, you as the individual have the ultimate say in how your life will turn out.

In another sense, you are what you hang around 99.9% of the time. If you hang out with broke people, chances are you are broke or are headed down that path to be the next broke person. If you hang out with brainiacs, chances are you are either one of them or you will become one. One thing my peers have allowed me to do at this age is motivate others through my experience with them.

Whenever I get the chance, I tell people about the great things that I have seen in the world. I let them know that there is much more out there than what they believe. I vocalize much more than the average person. Then, it hit me. I was blessed with a gift. The gift I have is that I have the power to simply motivate people to become greater than what they are. This has led to me having a great career in the spoken word and public speaking markets. As I thought about this, I said to myself, why not be the person to lay a guideline on how to use that voice we all have to make a change in the way people think. Why not be that person who people point at and say, "That's the man that I want to hear speak. He can give me the tools to get where I need to be." Why just give back when I can teach and give knowledge?

With the P.E.E.R.S. five step system towards achieving greatness, you will see how your inner voice and what you do can affect your outcome in not just your life, but many people around you as well. Much like the friends we choose, it is truly a reflection of us. Your work ethic and what you are willing to do to succeed is a reflection of you.

By the end of this step by step guide, you will learn the tools of what it takes not only to speak powerfully, but to achieve greatness overall. No, I cannot tell you how to make 10 million dollars in six days. No, I cannot tell you how to take a garbage can and turn it into a Buick. That is not the purpose of this book. If you want to learn how to make money, go to a financial seminar. If you want to learn how to simply use the power of speaking and other means to make those around you greater at what they do, then continue reading this book. Just like the saying "a closed mouth doesn't get fed" is powerful. Remember that an open mouth can feed the world if the knowledge is nutritious.

If it's one thing we are severely lacking in this world it's motivating the next individual. The person you motivate today could be the person who inspires your children tomorrow. Allow yourself to be a gift to someone else. Open up your heart and mind for expansion so that you can give life to someone who may need it. Trust, I have learned that sometimes a simply "Hi" can change someone's whole thought process. Let us now begin our journey into making yourself greater than you could ever imagine.

STEP ONE: PLANNING

I think back to the time when I was just 12 years old. In my hometown of East Chicago, Indiana, Jr. High School was and still is 7th and 8th grade. I was a measly 5'3, 120 pounds of nothing. I had no facial hair, I was chubby and my head was the same size that it is now.

Hell, to be real, I came out of my momma's womb with a head the size of a watermelon. If you have ever seen my baby pictures, or if you ever do see them, you'd be amazed that I didn't fall over every time I stood on my feet. Let's get back to the story at hand. There I was on the first day of school. I was dressed in a full Tommy Hilfiger outfit (That was before I found out how he truly felt about black people). I was outside with my friends that I knew from Franklin Elementary School, trying to figure out the kids who I didn't know from Field, Lincoln and Washington Elementary. If they didn't go to the Boys and Girls Club or hoop with me at the Baby Park across the street from my my grandmother's house, I really didn't know them, nor was I fond of them.

Early that morning, before any classes started, I laid eyes on her for the first time. I won't mention her name, but my God she was gorgeous. She was the prettiest sight that I had ever laid eyes upon (Now it's my wife. Not her). I was more nervous than a hog having to make it to the other side of the road that was lined up with barbecue joints.

For the next few days, I talked about her to my friends and was sprung beyond belief. I really believe T-Pain's "I'm Sprung" song was written based on my infatuation with this girl. The days passed as I had hoped she wouldn't catch me staring at her. Then one day, I guess her brother had gotten wind that I liked his sister and he confronted me at school.

"Hey man. I heard you bothering my sister??" Honestly, I don't remember if he said bothering or like, but I know I was scared as all get out. I remember telling him that I liked his sister. I can't remember too much of how he reacted, but I know we became friends shortly after that. Hell, me and my dude still remain good friends to this day.

What I am trying to get at is that even though I liked her, I had no plan of how to get her. Now, when it comes to the most beautiful woman in the world, who is my wife Chaz, I laid out an extreme planning stage. I first met her on December 29th, 2011 at the University of California at Riverside. I was there for a poetry show hosted by some friends that I knew.

The crazy thing is that I was on a date with a woman from Los Angeles at the time. Deep down, she seemed a little bit on the Looney Tunes side, but she hadn't fully let it out yet (eventually she did). I eventually got up to perform one of my poetry pieces and I wooed the crowd with my usual aggressive spoken word antics. As the show wrapped up, me and the lady I was with prepared to go spend our night elsewhere. That's when my now wife walked up to me with a business card. There she stood, all 5'4, 120 pounds of her. She was indeed beautiful. She was with two other women, but I really wasn't paying them any attention as I had my focus on her and only her.

In my mind, I thought to myself "How do I get rid of this one that's here with me to get with that one that just walked up to me?," referring to my wife. Eventually, me and baby girl from L.A. had a falling out (Thank you God) and I hit Chaz up. We began talking as friends on Facebook and texting each other over the phone, getting to know each other better. I would tag her in some of her friends' statuses telling them to hook me up with her. She probably thought I was crazy and didn't want to give me any time of day (My wife would later tell me that she did think I was crazy). Eventually, when I landed in Guam a few months later, we continued to grow with one another and communicate our interest in each other and in life. Then, I had to plan out how I was going to capture her heart.

Trust, it was a very tedious process. I hit up a whole bunch of her friends, trying to map out a day for her. It started with random face book posts on my page, saying that I had something big planned for her. That went on for a few weeks. Then, I had one of her home girls pick her up from the house and take her to a secret location. That secret location was a spa.

I spent over $600 on rose pedals, full body treatments and all that. Deep down, I really didn't know if this would win her over. I told myself that if she didn't budge, well at least I got to do something nice for a woman who deserves it. $600 to me wasn't really anything as I was overseas pulling in crazy bank. When it all came to pass, she loved every bit of it and on July 7, 2012, our journey of love began. Over the next three years, we had your typical relationship of ups and downs. It was hard in the beginning as all we had was Skype, due to the distance. When I came home at the beginning of 2014, that's when we really had a chance to feel each other out, seeing that we only had 30 days of interaction the previous year when I flew back to California.

In the end, we survived all of the ups and downs. On September 5, 2015, we continued that journey by saying I do by the waterfront in San Diego. I will admit, I cried with my groomsmen. It wasn't just for the fact that I was marrying the love of my life. It was also because we had survived through everything to get to that point.

So many times we go into situations on a whim, not knowing where to begin. Every now and then it works, as we become successful with that opportunity. That only happens .1% of the time. The other 99.9% of the time, we must plan in order to succeed. This is the first step of the five step process. The letter P which stands for planning is simply where the dream begins. Planning, as simple as it may sound, is actually the most difficult part of this five step process. This is the beginning. This is the start of something new. This is the first time you put the key in the ignition of a car when you are 16 and you drive. This is the first time you boil the water before you throw those Ramen Noodles inside (Best bachelor meal ever). It is the most important step because it involves you taking the first step. It involves you taking risks.

In order to properly plan, the first tool you need is that light bulb that goes off inside of your head. If you don't know what I am talking about, it's simple. That light bulb is the idea of what you will create. When I first started writing books while living on the island of Guam, I had no clue where to begin. I literally sat in front of a blank computer screen for a few hours a day and did nothing. I stared at the computer so much that if it were human it would've thought that I was a stalker.

Eventually, a friend of mines from Oakland, CA informed me about a short story contest.

The rules of the short story contest were to write 1,600 words per day for your story. As I debated on what to write, I slowly took myself away from the rigors of thinking and simply looked within myself. My life would be an interesting tale I thought. And there it began.

I simply took what I had gone through for 28 years and used it to create a story that has sold thousands upon thousands of copies to this very day. "The Writer's Block" may look like a simple book to some. Too me, it is a testament of taking the first steps in achieving your dreams.

CREATION of the idea is essential. It gives you a basis of what to work on. If you were living 100 years ago and wanted to create a personal computer like Bill Gates eventually did, you would have to see the vision first. Most people want to see the vision, but they don't want it to manifest, simply due to the work that is required to go into it. The times that we currently live in are give me this, give me that and give me more. This is partially due to the technology we have. You don't have to work for anything anymore. When I came up in school, if we needed to research for a book report, we went to the library and checked out books. Google has now taken the place of actually reading fine print on recycled trees. Type in any word and you will probably get several different meanings and stories behind them.

Textbooks are also becoming things of the past as classes are now lined up with iPads for each student. The only ipad I knew was my notebook. Am I necessarily knocking the invention of the World Wide Web? No, not at all. The internet has become a great asset for us all, connecting the world like never before. At the same time, it has also become our worst enemy when it comes to learning.

The best learning you can achieve is what you learn about yourself when you create and put in the work to make your creation come to life. I wanted to create a book. I put in the work, time and effort. Now I have created multiple books with multiple lessons that people can enjoy. I wanted to create a great poetry scene on the island of Guam while over there. With hard work, diligence and making connections, I did that. From the end of 2013 until I departed in February of 2014, the island's poetry scene was amazing. That is all due to me seeing the vision and then making it manifest.

What you must remember is that not everyone is meant to see your vision. Most people will think you are crazy. You will have naysayers, haters or whatever you want to call them. Just remember that 242 banks thought three men were crazy when they wanted to sell coffee. Now, you can find Starbucks on almost every corner in every city of the globe. Hell, there just may be one in the Sahara Desert that we don't know about. All in all, go out and create what may change the world one day.

Ok, so now you have created this idea. You have it etched in your head and you are certain that you can change the world. It is time to continue with the planning phase. Where do you go from here? As you scratch your head like the common thinking man, you come up with the answer to that question. Remember how our mothers (I know mines did) always told us that the only dumb question is the one that is not asked? Well that is the second step in the planning phase. QUESTIONS??? The alphabet has A, E, I, O, U and sometimes Y. In the case of planning, it has when, what, where, who, how and definitely why.

For this, I will just use my stance as an author to best describe it. I want to drop another book project for the masses. The reception from the audience that I have garnered from my previous project is an astounding one. People really like my writings and the stories that they entail. They are hungry for more. So now when the next project comes around, I have to first create, which I stated earlier.

Now, the real deal questions come. Question number one is "When will I drop the project?" As an author of four previous titles, it is important that I space out my projects in a way to suit the reader. This is what I mean. I don't want to have back to back to back releases of three books in three months. Over saturation can actually cause me to lose fans instead of gain them. Over saturating the market never gives the audience time to enjoy one book. They will feel overwhelmed and may garner the feelings that they are being forced to read my literary works.

Take Percy miller, a.k.a. Master P for example. For my non hip hop heads, Master P garnered success by creating a $300 million plus empire with No Limit Records. He also branched off into clothing, electronics, sports and other business ventures. There is no doubt that he is to be commended for what he did. At the height of No Limit's success, any one my age can tell you that No Limit stayed in people's faces. It seemed like they had a new release coming out every three days.

As a teen growing up in the 90's, I thought this was the greatest thing since sliced bread because I always had new music to listen to. As an adult with a better understanding for how things work, I think it was crazy. I really never had time to enjoy one album. It was more of listen to this as quickly as you can because something new will be out in the matter of a week. For Master P it worked. For most of us it won't. Timing is critical!!! I repeat. Timing is critical!!! I have to carefully plan out my releases.

Personally, I feel that releasing a book every 6-8 months is a good time frame. A half a year is more than enough time to read a story. If the audience enjoys it, then they know they have something good that they will be anticipating. You have to release your idea at the right time or your whole creation may be a flop. Today's musicians do this all the time.

Me being black, I grew up on hip hop. I love it to the core. In my opinion it is the greatest form of music because it allows for so many different types of expressions (Ever heard of N.W.A.). Even the so called artists people say are hurting the culture, I love them as well. Each type of music has its own purpose. Trust me; I am not going to want to listen to T.I. when I am going into deep thought on how to improve the community around me. In the same breath, you won't hear me playing Talib Kweli when I am in the gym trying to get a fierce workout in. That is my Waka Flocka Flame time because I need to hear the gunshots, aggressive lyrics, cursing and the occasional **BRICKKKK SQUADDDD** to get me hype to pump some iron.

As we continue to dwell on these artists, a new artist with a few hit singles will not want to release his album on the same day as Kendrick Lamar, J. Cole or Drake. That would just be idiotic as they probably wouldn't see any major sales due to whom they are competing with. The people who they are going up against are symbolic and embedded in the culture. They, the new artist, are just trying to get their foot in the door.

You have to study your competition, your audience and see what the logical thing is to do. Most planning points don't require in depth thinking. They simply entail using common sense. Another prime example is the movie industry. As we seen in the summer of

2015, Straight Outta Compton blew everything else out of the water when it was released. Any filmmaker with a right state of mind would see that it may not behoove of them to release their title on the same day as a movie they know will do major numbers.

Even when Lionsgate "Saw" franchise was big, no smart movie director would plan their horror film release on the same day as that. They would maybe release it a few weeks ahead of time, maybe even the month prior. Releasing it on the same day was not an option.

Do you get the point now? You have to really research the time you will put everything out as it can make the difference between your idea becoming a success or a complete failure. The next question is what and there are many what's to deal with. What impact will your idea bring to the world? What are the benefits of what I am doing? What are the negatives about it? What can be the consequences if my idea doesn't make it? What if your idea does make it? You have to take all of this into major consideration. All of these questions must be asked. Let us start with the first. What impact will your idea bring to the world? You have to really think outside of the box when it comes to answering this question. I have run across people wanting to do so many things in life. I ask them what impact will their creation have and the first thing that comes out of their mouth is something along the lines of

"Well, it's going to be something that everyone can use." To some that sounds like a logical answer. An in depth thinker however will hear that and still have no clue as to what impact it will have. Let's look at a can opener. It can open metal lids on cans. That is all fine and dandy. That still doesn't let me know what impact it will have on the world. Now let's look at when we ask the question of what impact will it have on the world with outside of the box thinking. The answer is that it allows for a can to be opened faster, safer and it will cut down on food preparation time. With that explanation, we now have a clear cut analysis of what impact the can opener will have. Over time, the can opener has evolved from turning it with your hands to electric openers with magnets and motors, which require you to do nothing at all but place the can in its position. That's the impact that I am talking about.

Aside from authoring books, I am an avid motivational speaker. Sure, I can go into a room and give a simple speech on how to improve your life with proper choices. If my presentation is off, I cannot connect with the crowd or if my presentation is just basic with sayings people hear every day, then I have had no impact.

Public speaking is an occupation where there is no room for error. You have to lock in the crowd within the first thirty seconds. If not, then you will be rambling on to a bunch of people who just want to go to sleep. They will probably be thinking about making a ham sandwich while you are still on stage talking. I learned this lesson in the Navy. Back in 2011, I was slated to take a three week course on becoming a certified instructor. I thought my poetry background and the fact that I love to talk would have me breeze through the class. After my first initial presentation in front of the class, I truly learned that I sucked. What I seen and what my instructors seen were two totally different things. I saw perfection. They saw a young man who needed a lot of help and guidance before he was ready to take the next step.

Once I got off my high horse and allowed myself to learn from those who had done it, I became not only a better teacher, but a better person overall. Okay, so let's move on to the next question of

"What are the benefits of what I am doing?" I'll stay on the speaking topic since that is where I last left off. When I give any motivational presentation, the benefits work both ways. For me, I benefit in several aspects.

One, the feedback from the crowd shows me what I need to improve on or what I need to increase. 99% of human communication is non verbal. It is easy to tell when you have a crowd in the palm of your hands. Even when you have given a great speech, you still have room for improvement. Aside from the crowd, a lot of that improvement will occur through self analysis. We will speak on the self analysis topic later. This is just one of many benefits that I obtain. As far as the crowd goes, let us take a look.

One, the quick benefit for them is hearing a great speech that motivates them to do great things.

Two, their confidence is boosted to be able to lead. When you analyze a great speaker, you analyze someone who has taken command of the room they are in and the audience that they are addressing. The audience gains important lessons on the subject the speaker is talking about. In addition, they also learn important lessons on how to conduct a presentation through observation. Again, they learn how to conduct a presentation through observation.

To see is to believe, and knowing something works for a fact can only enhance the person or people who are trying to learn. In general, humans need benefits from a product, service, a person or whatever it is that is being provided. If there is no benefit, then there is no reason to do it. In the corporate world, medical and dental benefits are a huge part of whether or not people will work for certain companies. Let's be real 100% right now. America robs and rapes people when it comes to Medicare.

If it wasn't for my military career, I would have paid over $50,000 for my knee reconstruction surgery in 2006. I don't even want to imagine what the cost was for my heart ablation procedure back in 2010. This is the only country that claims to have freedom of almost everything, but yet we really don't. We pay for everything with a consequence.

Even the freedom of speech that we have comes at a price (google Kanye West). That's why truthfully; I could never get mad at athletes or celebrities for some of the things they say. We all say the same things they do, except there isn't a camera in our face 24 hours a day. We are one in the same when we really sit back and think about it without bias.

Key word, without bias. Benefits are major when it comes to your success and here is why. We need to feel as if we are gaining an advantage. We need to feel as if our life and daily routines will become easier. There is someone who is reading this book hoping that they have an easier time in preparation for success. They are hoping that this book will give them instructions and lessons that will lead to their breakthrough.

Those are the benefits that make us want to learn. Now we reach the question that most people fear. What are the negatives? Everything and I mean everything has some negative connotation attached to it. Even the kindest, gentlest person on earth has something about them that others may not like.

Using myself for example, some people cannot stand me for my sometimes cocky nature. I am at times brash. I sometimes use foul language to get my point across. I am very stubborn at times. I am the type of person who commands attention whenever I walk into the room. Don't mistake this for me being an attention whore. I am not taking daily selfies and putting them on social media, hoping that everyone just loves how my face and body look.

When I say I command attention everywhere that I go, it all goes back to my demeanor. The way I dress, walk and talk, it takes people by storm in a way that they have no choice but to pay attention to me. To some, that is a negative, simply because they don't possess my qualities, or that isn't how they operate.

With the good comes the bad. You have to prepare yourself for that and know how to respond to negative criticism. Computers are probably the best thing I can think of. You love how they make life easier, but you hate how they can crash or go slower than an earthworm through the soil.

If you aren't ready to take negative heat for whatever it is you do, then you probably need to spend more time building your spine up before you step into the real world. The world as we know can be unkind at times. Being sensitive to dire remarks will have you doubting yourself faster than the Raiders chances of winning the Superbowl. I once performed a poem about love at a show. Now you would think that saying a poem about love would draw nothing but lovely smiles and blushes from the girls. I was wrong. After leaving the stage, this lady came up to me and voiced her displeasure with the piece that I recited. She had some terrible experiences with love and she felt that I rubbed it in her face that she would never find love again.

I didn't know this young lady, nor was I taking a shot at her. It just so happened to be one of those instances that my words were taken in a negative connotation. And truthfully, that's okay. If everyone is agreeing with what you say or do, then you aren't doing it right. The last two what questions truly define what type of person you are.

What if my idea does or does not make it? Some of you are probably thinking if your creation makes it, then you have reached success. I hate to inform you that this is terribly wrong. As humans we have a short attention span. What is here today is gone tomorrow in our eyes. Look at the infomercials on television. One week, the snuggie is advertised. The next week, it's the sham wow. The next week it is something else. Humans are always looking for the BBD. The bigger better deal. You have to ensure that you keep up or you will get left behind.

If your idea does not make it, do you just give up? Do you sit in the house for days just pondering on what if? Do you do that, or do you kick yourself in the rear and tell yourself "Its time to go back to work."

My deceased father in law was a principal in the inner city Los Angeles school district. Every morning he told his kids that it was time to go to work. That holds especially true when things do not immediately go your way. You must continue on the presses. The only thing being successful or unsuccessful does is either fuel your drive to continue on or it makes you complacent, which in turn sets you up for failure. Do you see where I'm getting at? As a thinker and creator, you will also have to ask yourself

"How to do I consistently improve so that people won't forget about me and what I do?" When writing my books, I upgraded with each one. I studied each project and judged myself fairly. I went into deep analysis on how I could improve each time. I graduated from the short story genre and went into a full length novel with my book BANDAGES.

From there, I progressed to a different story line with Sleeping with the Lights On. BANDAGES 2 was a sequel to the first, yet it still entailed a completely different story than the previous book which made it unique. So you see, with each book I wrote, I gave the reader something different. Yes, they are all urban fiction novels, but each one is unique in its own way. Each one has a different set of emotions, vibes and feelings. Unlike many authors who write in the urban fiction genre, each one of my stories don't deal with the cheating wife or husband, drug dealer, boss bitch or whatever other typical story line that plays out inside the ghettos of America. My books are stories which capture the mind and actually teach lessons besides who is sticking it to whom in the bedroom. Saying the same thing over and over will diminish the quality of not only the art form, but the authors who indulge their time, blood, sweat and tears into that art form.

You have to constantly improve. Being comfortable and complacent are the two easiest ways to fall off the map quick. People always want bigger and better as I said before, so you have to be willing to think bigger and better. You have to be willing to step out of that comfort zone you know and risk it all. You have to look in the mirror and tell yourself that you will be different than the rest.

Staying in the same lane as everyone else will do nothing but get you caught up in a mental traffic jam. The fork in the road may sometimes seem like a road that leads to nowhere. In the end, it may just lead to a huge mansion on the top of the hill. The road that everyone else takes may just lead to a collapsed bridge where they all fall off and die. When you ask yourself how you can improve, answer that with making your own footprints in the sand. The next question is why. Why am I doing this? If we want to talk about simple answers, this question embodies it.

Don't get me wrong; in a lot of cases, the answer is simple. You ask some kids in high school why they want to play football. They will straight out tell you it's because they want to hit people. That answer is straight, to the point and doesn't need much questioning behind it.

You ask people why they like to cook. They may say because I like to eat. Sure, that is simple and straight to the point, but unlike the previous question, it shows no main objective. When you think of football, you think of hitting. When you think of cooking, you think of many variables. We all eat, and we don't have to cook the food that we eat to get a meal. There are a million fast food joints, high quality restaurants, mom and pop joints, and wings-n-things (My favorite. Sorry Wing Stop) to quell the hunger of our stomach rumblings. Cooking however has numerous amounts of meanings. When you cook, you create. It is your masterpieces on the stove that will make someone else feel good. Cooking allows you to experiment, dibble, dabble and try new things that you may like or dislike in the end.

Cooking connects people. Look at the barbecues we have over the holidays. People will come together for some barbecue in a heartbeat. That is the aspect of cooking. It has many variables and results in many things. So when you ask yourself why you are doing something, it has to be more than just a simple answer.

I don't write books for myself to read. To tell you the truth, once my books are published, I do not read them. The only times that I read my books are after the final edit, just to ensure that no other grammatical errors are present. I write because I like to create stories that people can relate too. I write because I want people who haven't experienced an urban environment to feel like they are actually there. I write so that people can enhance themselves at reading. That right there is the biggest key in me writing. I want people to read. Reading is so underestimated in this world. No one wants to read anymore. We get so indulged in radio and television that we simply have forgotten how good it is to pick up a book. Whenever you think reading is less important than television, just remember what TV is called.

It is called television programming. You are being programmed visually while being told (hence the word tele. Pronounced Tella) what will program you. I challenge some of you to do what I am about to tell you. I learned this from comedian Eddie Griffin who has a level of knowledge that is very much under appreciated.

For one week (or longer if you'd like), put the television remote away. Don't cut on the television for anything. Simply read books about the history of your people, the world, science, and math, anything that will enhance your mind. Read the local and national newspapers so that you will stay in tuned with what is going on around you. I guarantee that you will feel like a totally different person once you are done. And some of you are asking how this can help me in being successful. It's simple. It allows you to get out of your comfort zone. In order to do what you aren't used to, you have to break from what you are used to. It is not that hard when you really think about it. All it takes is a bunch of good disciplinary skills, maybe some prayer and a whole lot of drive. Trust me, we all have it in us. It's our decision whether or not we want to pull it out of us.

The question of where now comes into play. This one isn't tricky as it may seem.

Where do I release or show off my idea? This is probably the easiest answer you will ever hear from me. You expose your creation to people that don't know you. Often times, we have a lot of yes people in our lives. Just because they know that you are a good person, they will tell you what you want to hear. You could have the worst idea on the planet. I'm not talking about a possibly impactful idea. I'm talking about one that doesn't make any sense at all. You could tell a lot of people in your circle that you want to pick up road kill and sell it on eBay. Sure enough, you will have some friends tell you that it is the greatest idea that they have ever heard.

If you have friends like this, remove them from your life please. They are not helping you progress. They are keeping you stagnant. They are simply known as the yes people and they offer you nothing but false hope. Going to people who have no idea who you are is beneficial because you will more than likely get straight forward answers. If you showed 100 people something and 89 didn't buy into it, then you may need to do work.

On the other hand, you may have something, but only 11 people dug it at the time. With numbers like that, however, I would advise you to keep going. Now, find another 100 people. If this time 85 out of 100 like what you are doing, then maybe you need to start preparing yourself to market in hopes of getting 85 more people to like your idea. Then progress all the way until you get the 100 you want. You can only go up from there. Whatever you do, just remember, the unknown will make you known.

Now that we have made it past the initial creation stage and the questions that you must ask yourself, we have to put the plan into effect. The third step in the planning phase is **LAYING THE BLUEPRINT.** On September 11, 2001, entrepreneur/rapper Jay-Z dropped a classic album entitled The Blueprint. It can clearly be put in the top 10 greatest hip hop albums ever made. From the opening title of "The Rulers Back," to the infamous Mobb Deep and Nas diss "Take Over," it clearly shined from beginning to end.

However, let's take an extra listen to Jay-Z and how he crafted the album. The title was more than a name. In each song, there was a different story. He went from Cocky (Ruler's Back), to cut throat (Take Over), to classic rapper (H.O.V.A.), to the playa type (Girls,

Girls, Girls), to self analysis (Song Cry), to lesson teaching (Renegade ft. Eminem). The first line of the song "Renegade" gives you a question to tickle your thought process.

"Mutha*****s/say that I'm foolish I only talk about jewels/do you fools listen to music or do you just skim through it." If that isn't a powerful line, then I really don't know what it is. Now, let's break it down. In this line, he is asking are you really listening to what he is saying. He claims that people say that he only raps about having big chains, watches and any other piece of jewelry known to man. It is clear that he views that as a negative when he asks the people "Do you fools listen to music or do you just skim through it?"

Now, what was the point of me breaking that down you ask? It was so that I can take you out of the inside the box mindset and start the process of having you think outside of the box. A blueprint is made up of several different parts that come together to form one great thing. In planning for greatness, you have to construct the blueprint of how you will reach that goal. Let's go back to my speaking career. Number one with me starts with just that. **ME!!!** I have to be confident in myself before I can start anything else. If you are fearful of the opportunity, then you will never achieve greatness until you defeat that fear.

Now, factor 1A is my dress game. It is a major element of my blueprint. When I am given the opportunity to do a major presentation through speech, I ensure that my clothes are on point. That means sharp creases in my jeans or slacks. The same creases will go in the sleeves of my shirt, whether it is a collared polo or a button down. My shoes will be well shined and buffed, giving me the highest professional look ever.

Even if I'm in tennis shoes or simple soft cloth Stacy Adams, they will be clean. No dirt or scuff marks will be present. Your appearance is the first thing that people notice about you. It is the first statement that you give you an audience that doesn't know you. If you look sharp, then more than likely you will be sharp. If you look like a bag of rocks, then more than likely you will get no one to pay attention to you. With dressing to the T, it is key to remember another point. You have to dress for the environment that you are speaking in.

If I am going to speak to a formally dressed crowd, I want to make sure that I blend in with similar dress. If I am going to talk to a group of young adults, I may want to relax my dress to something casual to avoid intimidation. Analyzing the crowd that you are going to entertain is essential when speaking or whatever you are going to do.

Ok, so now you are laced from head to toe clothing wise. What about everything else in between? The intangibles that we so vividly overlook can actually do more harm than good, so we must give extra attention to them.

Let's start with the hair. There are many forms of hair styles and hair types, but one thing is for certain. No matter how your hair is done up, it must present a neat appearance. A crisp, clean haircut tells a lot. Serving in the active duty military, our appearance is essential. The most however is the haircut. In the military, we hear more about hair regulations than any other regulation. They sometimes put more emphasis on haircuts than the darn mission. You have to keep your hair on point!!!

Men, that means nice fades, tapers or all evens. Even if you have dreads, ensure that they are neat looking and not ragged with hair frizzing out everywhere. Always have a crisp edge up. Black brothers know what I am talking about on this. The lining is the most important part of the cut. It keeps all the hair off of your neck, your ears and most importantly, it gives you a crispy clean appearance. Your lining should be so razor sharp that someone should be able to cut their finger on it to donate blood.

Moving down to the nose, it is imperative that nose hairs stay trimmed and out of sight. I never used to care about this aspect until one of my ex girlfriends complained about it many moons ago. We were talking one day and she said

"Babe, you need to cut your nose hairs. They are dangling out."

I really felt embarrassed. Here I was thinking I was smoother than a baby's ass, and I had hairs coming all out of my nose. I learned that you do not want to be engaged in a one on one conversation with anyone and your nose hairs are distracting them while you're talking.

After you have handled your nose, move your focus to the facial hair. Much like the hair on the top of your head, keep it well groomed and looking neat. Women, if you have a mustache, wax it off. Men are meant to have facial hair. Not women. I always edge my goatee up with a good razor lining. I trim it even so that all of the hairs are lying in unison.

There are some who like to have long, thick beards. That is fine and dandy as well. Just remember to treat it the same as you would a normal goatee. James Harden has one of the biggest beards you will ever see on the basketball court. Look at him closer next time you watch the Houston Rockets play. The top of the beard and mustache is well lined. The beard hairs are the same distance all around, making his caveman beard look like the thing to have. Now, look at your mouth. Keep those pearly whites whitened. There is nothing uglier or more of a turn off than seeing a mouth full of yellow teeth. People, this may sound funny, but stay close friends with your dentist. That man or woman can save you from a lot of embarrassment. If your teeth are crooked, you don't even need braces anymore as clear retainers have taken off. Ensure that you always have fresh breath, but never speak to anyone while chewing gum. It is a distraction and something that can turn a person who is interested in your idea away from you.

As a matter of fact, take a travel toothbrush with you. Before you go into a room to speak or handle business in general, go to the nearest bathroom and brush your teeth. A small bottle of Listerine will also come in handy as this will keep your breath fresh for a long time. As we move down, we reach the fingernails. I once had a bad habit of biting my fingernails. I mean I bit them so much that I only had nubs. On some occasions, I still catch myself nibbling on them like a twizzler. That is not an attractive thing to do as your nails can speak volumes about the type of person that you are to other people.

Your nails should be neat, trimmed and kept clean. Trust me, there are a lot of people who like to glance down and look at someone's hand when they shake it just to check the status of their fingernails. Some even look at dirty fingernails being equivalent to someone who came out of the bathroom after doing #2 and not washing their hands. In short, keep your nails in good order.

Ladies, please keep your natural nails or press on nails to a minimal length. Do not expect to conduct good business when you walk into the room with seven inch, multi colored nails. It is trashy, ghetto and a hot mess. Have more respect for yourself than that. I grew up seeing girls with that trash on their fingers. They thought they were cute when really they were making themselves look terrible. Don't downgrade yourself from women to rats. Now here comes the scenario that most aren't going to see as scary. What if the blueprint I made allows me to make it? There is someone out there thinking why I am asking this since I already asked the questions. It's different than asking the general questions that you have to answer.

Once you lay your blueprint out and things manifest, the ball game becomes totally different. If your idea or creation makes it, then you have succeeded. **WRONG!!!** You are more wrong than the NFL commissioner and his terrible antics that have deprived the game of football.

Congratulations, you came up with a concept that sparked worldwide interest and has the globe going. Let's say it's a brand new piece of technology. If you have seen the hit movie Kingsmen, that's where the idea just popped up in my head. Samuel L. Jackson created a computer chip that offered free service, but also caused people to kill each other to control the world's population. Now, of course your idea won't be as drastic as that (I hope not). Let's say you made a coat that the world was drooling over. This coat could adapt to any temperature and regulate your body heat. You had everyone wearing it from actors, ball players, singers; even the homeless people on the corner have gotten their hands on one.

You sold over 50 million coats worldwide. You think in your head that you have reached the pinnacle and have succeeded. However, when the buzz dies down and another coat or piece of clothing comes along, where do you go from there? See the biggest problem with ourselves is that a lot of us get comfortable once the blueprint has manifested. We achieve one goal and all of a sudden the work stops. There is no more progress. We are sitting on top of the world. If there is no more progress, then there is no more money. There is no more attention. There is no more talk of your sleek coat.

If you don't remember anything else, remember that achieving the goal is nothing. It really isn't. If a coat is a bad example for you, then let's take a look at the average Joe. Take a high school football player. His goal is to be starting on the varsity football squad. There is a lot of competition at his position, so it will not be an easy win for him. First comes the grueling weight room sessions. There is the waking up at eight in the morning to lift weights for two hours, just to get stronger. Once that's done, he has an eleven o'clock in the afternoon session of film study, followed by an hour of cardio.

That cardio includes running through cones, jumping over bags, wind sprints, bear crawls and up downs. All of these exercises are for the sole purpose of being in shape for four quarters and possibly more. Now, it's time to strap up the pads. The lifting has gotten him stronger. The cardio has made him faster and has given him stamina and endurance beyond measure. He now has to hit. He gets out there, ready for the full contact drills. His technique is great as he comes into contact with the runner. He is hitting, wrapping up and driving through with his legs. In 11 on 11 drills, he flies through the holes, stuffing the running back. He is flying past O lineman with a well orchestrated blitz that sacks the quarterback. After three weeks, the coaches have seen enough. They name him the starting outside linebacker for the team. He is happy as a pig in a pile of slop. He runs home to tell everyone of the good news. His mom, dad, sisters and brothers are all excited for him. Then the first game of the year comes. The lights are on, the crowds are pumped and kickoff is imminent. Here's the kickoff.

BOOM!!! His team stuffs the opponent's runner back at the ten yard line. He jogs out and is in the huddle. The middle linebacker calls the defense. **BREAK!!!** They break away and he lines up in his position. The ball is snapped, the full back comes his way, he meets him, but he can't shed the block and the running back goes 90 yards for the score. Do you see where I'm getting at with this? The kid's main concern was making the starting squad for varsity. That was all fine and dandy. But what did he do when he got that starting position? He simply blew it. That is what I am talking about being comfortable and complacent. You cannot just be satisfied when you have reached the goal. You have to keep pressing the issue. You have to keep working.

Remember one thing. When you reach one goal, there is always more work to be done to enhance the goal that you have already accomplished. Now, let's take a look at his situation a little bit differently as if his goal was successful. Let's go back to the first play from the ten yard line.

The ball is snapped, he drives the fullback into the running back and the team swarms on him, resulting in a measly one yard gain. He continues his great performance throughout the night. He ends up with 14 tackles, 3 sacks and a performance for the ages. The kid is tabbed as the next big thing. Congratulations, his goal has been accomplished. Now, is the work over? Absolutely not!!! When you finally achieve the goal, the same work must now be put forth day in and day out to ensure steady progression. I know I sound like a broken record but I have to beat this into your heads. It's good to have one good game. Now he has to have 10 good games in a row or more if they want to make the playoffs. When you set the bar high, you will see yourself perform at a high level, leaving no room for excuses. Also, it forces you to keep that bar high.

You upgrade, you don't downgrade. Look at how we drive on the freeway. When you are coming on to the freeway, you may be doing about 30. As you start to hit that open road and merge into traffic, your speed dramatically increases to 50, 60, 70 and then some. In the case of me, it's usually 90 plus, seeing that I am a speed demon on the road. I only slow down when I see a highway patrolman waiting on the side of the road.

My point is clear. You consistently must have a system of increase. Once you are on the decline, you either pick your speed back up or the fall will be a dramatic one. In today's world, with our here today gone tomorrow attitude, none of us have time to stay on a decline for long. There is always someone waiting in the wings to take your place. You have to decide whether you will be that number who is next in line or the number who is now out of line with nothing to give.

Planning it is the most imperative and essential part in achieving greatness. Without a plan, you take the chance of wasting the most valuable asset any of us have as humans. That is simply time. Time cannot be purchased back. There is no time machine to go back ten years ago and fix something you messed up. Time is more valuable than money. You can always print new dollar bills. You cannot reprint time and all the opportunity that you may lose.

STEP TWO: EXECUTION

When I hear the word execution, I automatically think of MACE, the fighting game that was out for Nintendo 64 years ago. When it was time to kill your opponent with the final blow, the voice on the screen would always say **"EXECUTE HIM!!!"**

This was my favorite part of the game as I got to use all the finishing moves I learned from magazines like Game Informer. I used to scream out loud whenever I finished off an opponent with a deadly move. I did the same thing when I use to play Killer Instinct from

Super NES and every Mortal Kombat known to man. Now, when I hear the term **EXECUTE,** I know it means to get the job done. That is the second step in the process.

EXECUTION, or simply getting the job done. When I was working on my book BANDAGES, I was riding the wave of success off of my first book The Writers Block. It was truly a jaw dropping feeling that I made people feel good with my words. The big difference between my first book and the one I was writing was the simple fact that I was now writing a full fledged novel.

This would be much different than having rules to guide you along when writing. I had to really think in depth with that project. There were many nights that I just sat and stared at my computer because I didn't know where to begin. Finally, I laid out a timeline on how I would get the book done. It went as followed.

- Dramatic Intro
- They meets someone
- Terrible interaction

- Lessons learned.
- An ending the reader will not expect.

I wrote these five notes down before I constructed the book. In the end, it helped BANDAGES become probably the best book I have written to this day. These notes simply laid the foundation for me to execute writing a novel. When actually doing the job, you will need assistance.

You cannot get around it what so ever. No one who has achieved anything great has done it alone. You can take Floyd Mayweather, Sugar Ray Leonard or any other great boxer for example. They had sparring partners, coaches who trained them up, cooks who prepared them the best meals, etc. All of those factors played a part in those great men executing in the ring. That is the first step of execution.

ASSISTANCE. It will take jotting down notes, people or some other means to be successful at what you do. When I get up to do spoken word or motivational speaking, I need the assistance of the MC. I need him or her to open my upcoming act with high expectations. Even if the people know me, there are those who don't know me and they need to feel good about me hitting the stage. Additionally, the crowd always needs a boost of some sorts.

Let's go to the squared circle. Professional wrestling is what I am talking about. True, it is sports entertainment, but the stunts that those guys perform are exceptionally real. If you don't believe me, just YouTube the guys who got hurt while performing in the ring. Mick Foley, better known as Mankind separated his shoulder, lost teeth and had numerous internal injuries after being thrown off a 20 foot high steel cage.

Shawn Michaels broke his back when falling on an oversized casket the wrong way. Stone Cold Steve Austin had his neck broke on a pile driver gone wrong. The list goes on and on. When those wrestlers come out to their music, there is an announcer who hypes them up. Fireworks go off once they make their way out from behind the curtain. There is a huge screen that shows highlights of them kicking ass in the ring. All this assists them in giving a better show to the audience. The crowd feeds off of it. It gets them ready to go for another big match. Just imagine if wrestlers came out to no music and no announcer. It would be one boring experience.

Now, we move on to the in ring action. Someone has to get body slammed. Both wrestlers know this, so they will prepare accordingly and assist each other in not getting hurt. The mat is basic wood and metal, so it isn't the best thing to constantly fall on. Notice how necks get tucked when hitting the mat? Notice how a wrestler bends his knees when he has to be lifted up? It is all a part of the process in assisting the other man to give the crowd a good show.

There has to be other valuables that add to your mystique and intrigue as a person. Even with new technology we see it. You don't simply see a new phone being advertised. You see a phone with this addition, that addition, etc. It has almost a million apps (not literally) that enhance the phone. There are so many other variables that make the new phone worthwhile and allow for peak interest from the consumer. Trying to do everything solo will not make your accomplishment bigger. It will simply make it harder to accomplish. Don't let pride get in the way of your success. You are never too good or too big to ask for help.

Alrighty. So now your execution is about to commence. The crowd is anticipating your creation as a game changer. Your invention, a remote that shuts up a husband or wife that talks too much (My wife would love that) is on the verge of setting the world on fire. The commercials (assistance) have advertised your product as the biggest blockbuster ever. The planning and preparation have led to this moment. Now comes the second and most important step of the execution.

SELLING. Have you ever heard the phrase of "Facts tell stories sell?" That is probably the truest statement ever created by man. What is going to sell whatever it is that you are trying to get through to the masses? Will it be your speech? Will it be your demonstration of the remote that has come to be known as the silencer? You have to think about this on a serious note. People are visual. Sure, it seems most of America is into what they hear and not what they see. You can see this everyday with people getting butt hurt by the things public figures say.

Visually seeing what can enhance your life is indeed a game changer. Take myself for instance. A few years ago I went car shopping. In my head, I was going to the car lot to purchase a Nissan Altima. I liked the design of the car from what I had seen on television and in person. My mind was locked and nothing would change my decision. That's what I told myself until I actually arrived at the car lot.

As I was walking through the lot, my wife stumbled across a Buick. Growing up in the Midwest, I remembered how it seemed all of the big time guys (drug dealers) drove big body Chevy's and Buick's. I loved those cars and once she spotted a Buick, my interest quickly went to that. Now I had a choice. Either get this Buick, or go with my first choice from jump. How did I come to the conclusion? I simply let the cars sell themselves with how they felt when I drove both of them. In the end, the Buick in my opinion drove much better. I rolled off the lot that day with my new baby I named BETA (Bee-ta), which is the same nickname of my nephew Darrell.

The same is true when it comes to the marketing of your product. What sells it is the key. You can present fact after fact after fact. If the facts don't sound great to have, then you will be just another person with a product that is sitting on a shelf. When you sell your product, ensure that you use all means to sell it. Social media, websites, billboards, word of mouth, getting your product in a celebrity's hands are all means of selling your product.

All of these are selling points that can result in you taking the next step towards greatness. Just remember, how bad you want it depends on you. The consumer can only buy into whatever it is that you are selling. You have to ensure they are sold on you. The third step of execution is one that scares people the most.

THE PRESENTATION!!! Oh boy. Let's think about all of the times people have talked our ears off. We all have that one friend who hits us with a barrage of stories in the club. They can tell you everything about every player at HOOTERS while watching the football game. Then comes the time where they have to talk to the masses.

All of a sudden...there is silence. You can hear the crickets chirping. You can hear a rat piss on cotton. You can hear a roach a mile away because they are ever so silent. That is the major problem with most of the world. Research shows that 97% of the world's biggest fear is public speaking. Let's do the math on this because that is a very high number. You take the world population which is about 7 billion. Okay, we will just mark it off at 7 billion. 97% of 7 billion is 6,790,000,000. That means that 6.79 billion people are literally afraid to speak in front of a crowd. That leaves a mere 210,000,000 million people who are not afraid of the public eye. In short, that is a very scary statistic. What do I mean by that? It's simple. That leaves 6.79 billion people who can't impact the world through speech. When you look at the history of the world, many upon many of leaders brought people together through mere words. Even when that purpose was evil, they brought folks together.

Adolf Hitler is a perfect example. The things that he did were indeed cruel and unjust. He was still able to lead masses upon masses of Germans to do his bidding. Malcolm X, who in my opinion was a way better leader than Michael King (some of you know him as Martin Luther), talked with supreme authority.

By any means necessary makes even the black children of today want to rise up and conquer the negativity that comes against them. Words have the power to casts spells upon people. That's why they call it spelling. The say words are powerful because they cause people to do things that they wouldn't usually do. Imagine if there was a woman who was always called ugly her whole life. Now, we will talk in the sense of her physical beauty. On a scale of 1–10, she is a 7.5. In the normal world, that isn't bad at all. She lives in the hills of Hollywood, or Hollyweird as I call it. We all know out there that plastic boobs, silicon butts and flashy jewelry are the norm. What if every man she encountered her whole life called her ugly simply because she was naturally built? You guessed it. She will think that she is ugly.

Then comes the one gentleman who sees her and tells her straight out that she is beautiful. Now her whole life and attitude about herself has changed. This can work two ways however. She can either truly believe that she is beautiful. Or, she will not believe it because she is so accustomed to people always saying that she is one ugly duckling. What we hear on a regular basis shapes us out as well. As with the woman's case, it works both ways for us. You can either accept it or reject it. I deal with it on a daily in the Navy. I have leaders (and I say that loosely) who can tell me something and I take it as okay, they are literally trying to help me. Then there are those who like to tell you things to boost their own ego, hoping that they break you down in the process. STRENGTH is the next key in the execution process. You have to be strong to handle whatever type of reaction you encounter.

I once performed a spoken word piece at San Diego's quote on quote premiere spoken word show. I won't delve too much into this place or the people who frequent it, seeing that I personally have a strong dislike for a lot of them except for a certain few. So I'm into my piece and a line I spit went like this

"yes your ***** has fallen off my radar like the Malaysian airline." As I was about to delve into my next line, a woman in the front quickly holla'd out

"Too soon. Too soon." Now, the ignat, East Chicago, Harborside hood raised hoodlum wanted to say off the grid words to her, but I had to remember that I was spitting for hundreds of others, so I couldn't let ignorance prevail. Instead I holla'd out a quick

"No it ain't" and continued on with the piece. You see in a time like that, you have to be strong. You can't let people bait you into a reaction that you may later regret. True, I don't regret anything I say. However, had I let out a "Shut up B***h" or "F**k your feelings," then a whole other crap storm would have been evolved from that. She would've got mad. I would've said I don't care. Here comes the boyfriend or husband, and now I have to kick his ass.

That's simply the power that age has. You handle things differently. Strength is essential when you speak. Let's go to a different scenario. What if you mess up? Of course, in public speaking, unlike poetry, you don't have to memorize lines. Your thought process can go awry at times like anyone else. That's when you remain at a calm level. There are several tricks to quell this.

One, keep a simple glass of water handy on a stool or chair. You'd be amazed at how a quick drink can bring you back down to reality and allow you to finish a great speech. Now, I have even seen some speakers in my day have alcohol while on stage. That speaker's name is Eddie Griffin (Here he goes again). Yes, even comedians are considered speakers. I don't recommend this, but for some people, it works. In his field, where cursing, slangin' jokes and roasting people are a must, then yes, alcohol is a good way to bounce back.

If you are just a general speaker, I recommend staying away from that. I am an avid Hennessy drinker. I can tell you that enough of that medicine will have me saying some off the wall stuff. Again, water is a common and recommended cure for this.

Secondly, you can reiterate a point. People don't usually mind hearing a quick repeat of something important. I am not talking about saying a whole paragraph over. I'm simply talking about saying one line (As I've done in this book). A lot of times when we hear speakers do this, it is to reiterate something. In the same breath, we hear a lot of speakers do this to be able to remember their next key point that may have slipped from their mind. The time that this happens to me the most is in my spoken word. If it's a new piece that I am performing for the first time, I usually enhance a major line with another spur of the moment line to bring myself back to a part I may have forgotten. If the rare occurrence happens where you forget everything you were speaking on, simply freestyle.

However, when you freestyle a presentation that was organized, ensure that you keep focus on the main topic at hand.

Third, to quell the loss of memory, have a short outline available on a stool or platform on stage. Do not constantly look down at it. Take a quick look to put you back on track and finish your speech.

Now that we have finished how to quell memory lapse, let's continue on with the execution process. We talked about selling your story and having strength while speaking. What is the last "S" you ask? That's easy. The last "S" is SIMPLE. You want to keep things simple. So many times we get so into making a big presentation that we get over excited. We want to have this prop and that prop. We want to talk about this and talk about that. We just want to blow our speaking presentation out of the mutha*****n water (Excuse my French. I got excited!!!) That is all fine and dandy. However, if we get too wrapped up in having a flawless performance, we usually end up creating more flaws.

When you keep it simple and stick to the basics, you perform well beyond what you thought you would. Watch the movie Varsity Blues when you get a chance. It is more than just a classic football film. It is one that has several different lessons in it if you pay attention. In one part of the movie, Coach Kilmer is with QB Jonathan Moxon at practice. He is upset with a play Mox is trying to run. After a verbal spat between the two, he hits him over the helmet with a whistle I believe and tells him repeatedly "Stick to the basics. Stick to the basics."

Well that holds more than true in the public speaking profession. Simplicity ensures that everything in your control goes smoothly. Don't spend time worrying about the lights, the microphone or the flooring of the stage. Worry about you. When you focus on yourself and getting yourself right, then and only then can you focus on other things.

In other words, before you can help someone else, you must help yourself. I see a lot of people making this mistake in life. They have the biggest hearts you could ever imagine. They are willing to give their last dollar to their fellow man just to see them eat. Yet they never think about how they are going to exist.

How can you feed a homeless man when you yourself have nothing to eat? How can you build someone a home when you don't have your own place to call a home? How can you teach someone how to add 2+2, yet you don't know basic math? You have to be at the pinnacle yourself before you can lead someone else to the pinnacle. And look at the word I just wrote.

LEAD. Realize, all of us aren't meant to be

leaders. Some people are meant to be followers. Is this saying that you sit back and not do anything? No. A great leader is made better by his followers. Followers play the most important roles in a leader's success. How many average wide receivers did Tom Brady have, yet he made them look like Gods on the field? That comes from true leadership. He allowed his surrounding teammates to trust in him, therefore making them want to increase their production dramatically. You see how this works now? Execution is a process. It is not just about getting the job done. It is also about making those around you better. If you aren't making anyone around you better, then what you are doing is pointless.

STEP THREE: EVALUATION

In the military, every year we have one main evaluation. It is basically a report of what we have done for the year and we are ranked against our peers. The same goes for civilian jobs, except it is done on a regular basis.

Everywhere you go, with everything you do, you will have an evaluation. Someone will always be watching over you, making sure that you are doing the right thing. If they see you doing the wrong thing, then you will either be corrected or fired. Evaluations will never go away no matter where we go in life. You see it in everyday life outside of the job. The police are a major evaluator. In the inner city, it is common for police to stop a group of young minority males and harass them. Now before I continue, this is not the police bashing post of this book. This is simply an observation that I made growing up. When in groups of three or more, police have a tendency to pull over, ask us questions and try to find something that is wrong. It is profiling and it is a problem that will probably never go away.

However, their evaluation comes from how a group of men are dressed or the particular building they are occupying. The most important aspect of evaluation however is self evaluation. It is the biggest part of being successful. It is more important than any of the other steps listed in this book. A lot of times, we as humans like to lie to ourselves. We have a tendency to believe that we are the best at what we do. In a sense, it is good to have that mindset, because if you don't believe you are number one, then who will?

With that thought process, however, you have to be real with yourself. When I first started performing spoken word in an old church on 25th street in San Diego, in my mind, I had a vision that I was going to woo the crowd. I thought my shit was going to be immaculate. It turns out that I could barely scratch the surface with some of the words that I was spitting.

I took a close listen to one poet in particular. His name is Deacon Blair. He had a unique style about him. He was a laid back cat, skinny, very mellow, but his words made him sound like Malcolm X. To be honest, he is the spoken word artist that I look up to the most out of all of the ones I know. He simply accepted who I was, never judged and continued to be a great influence on myself.

Once I heard him and some of the others, I knew that I had major work to do. More importantly, I was honest with myself and realized that I wasn't the best at what I did. From that 2009 year and beyond, I continued to listen to other poets. I analyzed them, observing what they did different than me. With many long nights in my bathroom mirror practicing and writing in notebooks, I finally mastered that art of performing spoken word.

No longer was I the person who was just expected to do something crazy like strip down to his shorts while performing (true story). I was expected to give powerful words that left a lasting impression. Hard work and diligence eventually landed me to my then biggest gig.

R&B singers Joe and Jon B. were slated to perform in San Diego on February 11, 2011. Through a hook up from my barber (James Threats. Love you mane), who was also a part time promoter, he set me up with the main promoters of the show and it landed me as the opening act for those two.

I clearly remember it like yesterday. I arrived at the Spreckles theatre in Downtown San Diego at around five o'clock in the evening. I met with the promoter who had booked me and relaxed backstage. As I sat back there waiting for a seven o'clock show time, I took in awe everything around me. The stage and theatre was empty. Five to six thousand seats were just waiting to be filled. I immediately thought to myself two things. One, it is an honor to be here. Two, what in the good hell am I really about to do?

I was use to crowds that numbered in the low hundreds. Thousands however? I hadn't crossed that threshold. The nerves started to kick in as the time winded closer to 7 p.m. I eventually found myself eating downstairs with Joe's band. I didn't talk to them at all. I sat at a completely different table trying to stay to myself. I was trying to get my mind right for what could be a make or break for my spoken word career.

Finally, the time came for me to perform. With about five minutes until the top of the hour, the MC for the night went out on stage and introduced me. As I walked out, I really couldn't see anything but the first few rows. After a quick introduction, I let loose. With every word, I was praying to Jesus not to let me screw up. This was my one shot at greatness. By the end of the piece, I got a major ovation and I retreated to the back relieved. I sat down in a chair just thanking God that I didn't mess up. My heart rate went back down and I retreated back to the crowd.

The rest of that night was more than amazing. I had one of my friends who didn't even know I performed poetry come up to me and just clamor in awe. Random people were telling me how great I sounded on stage. One girl even said that she would give me some ass if I got her backstage to meet Joe. As great as that offer was (Cause she was fine), I had a fiancée (not my current wife) at the time, so that to me was a no go.

February 11, 2011 changed my life forever. It was the day that I stepped out of being a local celebrity to a nationwide presence. It opened the doors for me to perform from Oakland to Texas. In light of all that, I went home that night with something else in mind. You would think that the first thing I did was just plop on the couch and smile. Instead, I attached the cable from my digital camera to my television and watched my performance. As happy as I was for that monumental moment, I deep down did not like it. It wasn't that I didn't do well. It was simply that I know I could have done better. On a scale of 1–10, I evaluated myself honestly and gave myself an 8. I strive to achieve the highest grade possible of anything that I do. An 8 to me is not acceptable. The lesson I am trying to teach is this.

One, **YOU CAN ALWAYS GET BETTER.** You should never be satisfied with one, few or many great performances. There is always room for improvement. The man who believes he has achieved a mistake free task is the one who is setting himself up for failure. You will always make mistakes no matter how great you become at speaking or anything else.

Even Michael Jordan never shot 100% every night. He missed a lot of shots, particularly game winners. Pippen didn't steal every ball that came his way, even though he was a defensive guru. Rodman didn't grab every rebound that came off the rim, even though he is the greatest rebounder in the history of the NBA. We can never be perfect, but we can always get better. That is the major point of self evaluation. Telling the truth to yourself before anyone else has the chance too. Lying can only send you down a path of clear destruction.

As we talk about self evaluation, I feel it is necessary to share my own story to my readers so that they can feel closer to me. The road leading up to me and my wife's marriage wasn't a smooth one. I would lie to myself, saying that I was a good boyfriend. In a sense I was. In another sense, I didn't want to face the fact that at times I would want to chase after other women. I had times where I just belittled her and made her feel like the lowest person on Earth. I felt like she was trying to do so much wrong to me, that I felt the only way to make myself feel good was to make her feel like she was nobody special. I made her cry many of nights. I threatened to break up so many times because I just felt I couldn't take her mess anymore. When the time got closer for me to get engaged to her, I started to realize that the majority of the problems we faced were caused by me. I had to look in the mirror and ask myself who was this man. It surely wasn't the man that my parents raised. It wasn't the man who she met in the beginning.

Once I finally had the balls to face myself, it started a trickle effect inside of me. Slowly but surely, I came back to the man she loved. More importantly, I came back to the man that I loved being. So to end this paragraph, I say to the whole world that I apologize to my wife for all of the unnecessary things I put her through. If you are a young man reading this, learn a lesson from me. I almost messed up something great. Had I not ended up with my wife, I would still be lost in this world. Don't think you are immortal and she will stick around because y'all are both young and not fully matured. She just might mature faster than you, realize what she is going through and bounce. Then you will be the one begging for her back with late night calls. Remember, old fools used to be young fools.

I have so many associates who have aspiring dreams to become rappers. They feel just like the next man. They feel as if they are one hit away from stardom. They dream of walking the red carpet at the BET awards or becoming the next rapper to win an Oscar (shout out to Eminem and Three Six Mafia). This is cool and all. I commend them for attempting to live out their dreams. In reality, a lot of them aren't honest with themselves.

When you listen to their music, they sound like every other artist that is out there. When I say every other artist, I am not talking about J. Cole, Kendrick, Eminem, Nas, Jay-Z or any of those types of artists. I'm talking about your everyday club bounce, drill, trap, gangsta or catchy rhyme type rappers.

What is a catchy rhyme rapper you ask? We all know who those are. Those are the guys who make a song with a good beat and a hook that you can't do anything but sing because it is so catchy. This leads me to another step in the evaluation process. You need to ask yourself **WHAT SEPARATES ME FROM EVERYONE ELSE?** When I go to any spoken word venue, I always make sure that I am up on the times at hand. Myself, I tend to stay away from what I call "The trending topics." Social media has an amazing way of making and keeping things relevant for ungodly amounts of time. Poets have a knack to want to be the first to write on the trending topic at hand, thinking that they are the only ones who will speak on it. Then when they realize everyone is saying the same thing, all of a sudden it becomes "I have to say it better than he/she does."

Take the Eric Garner case for example. Now, this part of the book is the police bashing post. I am very much appalled with the NYPD. I'm not even from New York, but I can tell you from their history, I personally believe that they are a bunch of crooked asses who think they are gangstas. I really feel like they are a bunch of guys who didn't get laid at a young age, got bullied in high school or they have no authority in their homes because they try to bully everyone they see. That includes a former #4 ranked tennis player in the world who did nothing but wait outside of a 5 star hotel for a limousine to take him to the U.S. Open. All that because he was black and "supposedly" looked suspicious. What they did to Eric Garner was beyond malicious.

We all saw the tape. We all heard the man saying he can't breathe. We all saw him lying dead on the concrete while they were trying to figure out what BS story to come up with. Now, I know right now, some people are probably putting the book down. Some are probably calling the local talk shows, CNN or any other controlled media platform to say "OMG, look at what he wrote." By all means go ahead. I have learned over time that no one is ever going to be happy with everything you say. Even when you say good morning, some people are going to get pissed off because they are grumpy. I'm pretty sure there are some Klan books out there that say screw black people, Jews and whoever else. The difference between me and the majority is that

I don't get offended. If you say my name, then we can talk to each other. I don't answer to subliminal shots or snickering. I operate by name dropping. That way you all know exactly who I am talking about. Now, let's go back to the subject at hand.

When the Eric Garner tragedy happened, I could go on YouTube, any social media site or attend any poetry venue and here at least four poets that night come with an Eric Garner piece. The frustration is there and I get that. I commend them for speaking up against such injustice. When you really sit back and think about it however, it's all cookie cutter. In speaking, you have to differentiate yourself from everyone. It's not cool when everyone is the same. It is especially not cool when everyone is the same type of person at the same time. If we were all the same, the world would be totally boring. Imagine, just imagine for a quick second if everyone in the entire world was worth 100 million dollars. I mean really think about it. We all are born with 100 million dollars. With that type of wealth, who would work? The answer is no one. There wouldn't be any grocery stores. No construction companies. There would be no anything that brings value to our lives. If every single one of us was rich, why would we labor? Everyone has a role to play. So when I know a hot topic will be broadcast across a stage, I avoid it. It gives the audience a breather when they hear me speak. Trust, an injustice is an injustice, but no one wants to head to a venue to hear 20 political pieces on the same thing.

Separation is what really makes a speaker great. Separation allows your audience to embrace the unique qualities that you may only possess. If we are all the same, then again, we would all be boring. So in turn, I guess the NYPD being known as a bunch of bullies is a good thing. Without the bad cops, we couldn't appreciate the good cops like Indiana State Trooper O'Bryan Winfield. Hammond (IN) police officer Jonathan Woods. We couldn't appreciate the thousands of other cops who lace the boots up every day and actually uphold the motto to serve and protect. The same goes with the military. For every great sailor who acts accordingly, there is a sailor who brings dishonor to themselves with wrongful actions. When I tell some people who have never served that we deal with gangs, drug addicts, alcoholics, rapists, child molesters, murderers and other horrific people, they look at me in shock. They say

"No, not in this great country's military." Yes, in this great country's military, many of the problems that plague the world happen right behind the security fences as well. Just as I talked about the police, I'll talk about the profession I'm a part of. We aren't immune to being different, nor being terrible people at times. I have done a lot of things in my military career that I am not proud of.

I have been drunk in public overseas. I have yelled obscenities on top of a table with a bunch of sailors cheering me on (And y'all got pissed at Jamies Winston while he was at Florida State. HA). I have been involved in overseas brawls (Australia and Hong Kong). I have had nights where I was with a group of sailors running from the police (Singapore). See even with all the negative talking I did about the police, I came back to myself. This man here will never admit to being the model citizen all the time. This goes back to the real self analysis that I was talking about earlier. It even goes to a bigger point here with **REVEALING YOUR FLAWS**.

We sometimes get to a point in life where we feel that we have it made and try to sweep every negative thing we did under the rug. What I have learned in speaking is that the audience isn't more captivated by the success story. They are more captivated by learning that you are the normal human. You are flawed. You make mistakes. You have been beaten down and got back up.

When I talked to a group of young adults in Palm Springs back in August of 2015, I revealed the dark past that I had. I grew up in a broken home. I hustled moonshine (illegal). I associated and ran with the Gangster Disciples. I felt no love from anyone except for a select few people. I was a broken person. In the words of a good friend of mines, Gill Sotu, I was a flawed American male. Seeing the looks in those young adults' eyes was truly humbling. Knowing that I came from the same background as some of them and made it, it garnered their attention even more. See public speaking is more than just talking a bunch of juju to an audience. It is really about opening up your soul. If you aren't willing to open up and expose who you truly are, you are doing more damage to yourself than you are doing to the audience that is listening to you.

When you add two negatives, they always make a positive. The times in your life that you want to hide in the darkness will always come to light. The key word in that is light. Light symbolizes life and life is always brought out of darkness. Think about babies and when they are born. They are in a dark place inside of their mothers. Once they are pushed out, they come into the light and cry, solidifying their birth. Look at where you came from to where you are now. If you have progressed to do great things, consider yourself reborn.

STEP FOUR: REPEATING

Over my lifetime, there are some things that I have gotten tired of doing. One is partying every single weekend. When I first arrived in California, it was tough. I had no car, no phone or no family. All I had were a few outfits and a ship to call home.

Over the next two months, I walked everywhere and rarely left the Naval Base. My fun was confined to a recreation center, the gym and the bowling alley. After what seemed like forever, I had a friend named Phil who was in the same predicament as me. He rented a car and we rolled on out to see San Diego for the first time. I remember every detail of that day. I had on a New Jersey Nets all red jump suit. We were in a red car. Phil had on a red shirt. As we parked somewhere downtown, we stopped for a minute.

"Man I hope they don't think we Bloods," he said. I hadn't thought about it until he said it, but he was right. We were draped in red. I didn't know if this city was all Bloods or all Crips (I would later find out that San Diego was a Blood city). Nervous was an understatement. Where I was from, we didn't have Bloods or Crips. The colors thing was brand new to me. All in all, we ended up making it back to the base that night unharmed, but I learned a valuable lesson. I would never in my life do that again. I would research wherever I went to avoid unnecessary situations.

Over the next ten years, my wardrobe changed to any color that wasn't red or blue. I constantly repeated the lesson I learned on that day. And this brings me to my next step in striving for greatness. **REPEATING or RE-**

DOING. Once you have made the leap into becoming a success, you have to repeat what you did before in order to continue your drive to the top. Look at some of the greats in sports. Barry Bonds was a 7x MVP. Bill Russell was an 11x NBA champion. Yogi Berra won an astounding 10 titles with the New York Yankees.

These great gentlemen, regardless of your personal feeling towards them, repeated the same powerful work ethic that got them all of those accolades. With speaking, writing or whatever you do, once you have found out what it takes, it must be constantly repeated. You may have to change with the times, but never change the formula that works. I repeat, **NEVER CHANGE THE FORMULA THAT WORKS!!!**

But Joe, you just said you may have to change with the times. Let me clarify my remarks on this. I have a formula that has allowed me to have success in what I do. That will more than likely never change. I have changed with the times however. When I first started, I didn't have a website. I realized that I needed my own platform. A place where people could go to learn more about me and what I do (www.joemacuncut.com). So, I created one. When I first started out in poetry, I would cuss every other word almost and do crazy antics that made the crowd remember me.

Now, I don't have to do that. I have learned to diversify my words. I have learned that words are more powerful than any action you could ever do in regards to spoken word. When I began writing, I had a plan to write all urban fiction novels. With the times we are living in now, I felt like I had to shake things up and step out on faith to help the masses.

I am still sticking to the great writing formula that has taken me far. I have though changed with the times so I can give motivation to people who may need it. I consider this book the "To Pimp a Butterfly" version of the book world. No one expected Kendrick Lamar to come with the material he did on To Pimp A Butterfly. I don't believe anyone expected me to come with a motivational and life coaching book either. His singles "Alright" and "Blacker the Berry" speak on the tough racial times we live in as black men. This book is a result of seeing those same black kids struggle with the thought that they will never achieve anything great. That's truthfully why I wrote this.

Does this relate to any and everyone? Yes it does. I just want everyone to know that the poor kid who was never told anything positive in life is what motivated me to write this. I was once that kid who was listening to Indiana Pacers forward Antonio Davis speak life into us youth at the Boys and Girls Club in Gary, Indiana. They are my favorite team and I was more than intrigued that day.

Now, all I am doing is repeating the process. Repeating the process. Life is a constant cycle. It can be one of great honor when we teach positive things to someone the way we were taught. We all couldn't be born with a silver spoon, but we can teach all how to obtain a spoon so they can eat. Notice how throughout this book how I have repeated many sayings and phrases, trying to beat them into the heads of the millions who will read this. If we don't repeat the positive things that got us where we are, then we are simply bound to repeat the negative. Look at all the NBA players who have gone broke after earning millions upon millions of dollars. It's because they repeated the negative choices with their money. They purchased fancy cars, clothes, jewelry, five or six homes, $50,000 parties and all other sorts of nonsense.

Let me not even start to talk about those who tried to take care of everyone and their momma. I wonder where those people are at when they go broke. I can tell you that they are nowhere in sight. Once the money leaves, they are gone as well. We see this example on a regular, but many choose not to heed the warning of those who messed up before them. They repeat the same mistakes. It goes both ways. Let's get into a personal story of mine using both sides of the repeating process. The positive side and the negative side. For a long time during my younger years, I constantly made a choice to repeat foolish mistakes. I was ripping and running the streets. Girls were my weakness. Partying was my major weakness. One night, that repeat cycle got to me. I went to a party in a well established area of San Diego. Out there, you didn't have to worry about gun shots or people just trying to start mess with you for no reason. I got to the party with a friend, not knowing anyone else in the house but him. I was just mere days from my 22nd birthday.

I thought hey, what is the worst that could happen. I am in a good neighborhood with some sexy women, so everything should be good to go. The night went on without a hitch for the most part until I met a girl outside. I was completely oblivious to the fact that she had a boyfriend, so I thought I was doing no wrong. It turns out that the whole time we were outside talking, he was staring a hole through both of us. As we entered back into the house, he called her over giving me the side eye and I walked into the living room to see a "freak" contest going on. Now at age 21, I considered this the life. I had music, women, some drink and a peep show going on in the living room. So how could anything go wrong? I had spoke too soon as the host of the party's boyfriend was caught upstairs having sex with someone else.

That was problem number one. Problem number two occurred when my friend was caught upstairs with another guy's girlfriend. That's when all hell broke loose. My string of partying like it was no tomorrow was about to come to a crashing end. As I stood in the back yard with my friend and other brothers, we saw one of the guys pull out a gun from his truck. I thought to myself

"Damn. I am about to die." As you can see, I am writing you this book and am still alive. However, the events of that night that followed forever haunt me to this day. The man eventually pulled off with his girlfriend in his truck. As I recall a young woman on speaker phone listening to the conversation between the crazed man with the gun and her friend in a truck, I clearly remember the sound of metal turning and crunching against the street. My heart literally stopped, as did everyone else's for that matter. My friend ran to his car as I hurried behind him. We sped through the streets of San Diego hoping to find them.

What we came across just mere minutes later solidified the fact that I needed to slow down with my life. In the middle of the street lay a young lady, bleeding from all over. Two men sat off on the side of the road looking un-phased by the accident. The scene went from 0 to 100 real quick. The young ladies at the scene attempted to fight the men. I on the other hand was concerned about this young lady in the middle of the street.

I took my shirt off on that hot summer night and placed it over her body. She was losing more blood with every passing second and I did what I could to at least give her a chance to survive. By the time the paramedics and the ambulance came, the scene was more than hectic. I stood off to the side to avoid the ruckus, but I couldn't escape it. My partner drove me to the party so I was only leaving at his discretion. We made it to the hospital that night and stayed there until literally six in the morning. I gave my grandmother a call back home in Indiana to let her know that I was okay. I had the decency to do this before she received grandma's intuition in a dream of some sorts.

As I sat in the waiting room, listening to tales of who was going to kill who, I began to unravel inside. I took some time to myself and walked outside. By the time eight o'clock rolled around, my mans was ready to go back to his crib. The stay didn't last long as we later jumped in the car with three other men. All I will say is that by 12 that afternoon, I was sitting in a car outside of a house with three other guys who were all strapped.

The guy in the house they were after had guns as well, so it was a no win for both parties. That incident is what stopped me from always wanting to go start and end the party. I had repeated this process for the first three years of my life in California. It had finally caught up to me in a way that I never wanted again. Over the next few years, I continued to party, but I made adjustments as necessary so that I wouldn't find myself in that predicament again.

One, I always made sure that I drove myself anywhere.

Two, I only went to parties where I would know multiple people that had good sense inside of their cranial.

Three, I didn't go anywhere in which I had to question why was I going there. The repeat pattern of stupid decision making was no longer repeated. I now had a new plan and it saved me from a lot of mess over the next couple of years. Fast forward to my life now and a positive repeat process.

As I sit in my beautiful home in the hills of California that looks over to other homes on a higher hill, I smile and reflect. I repeated a pattern of smart work to get where I am at today. Who would ever think that a young black male from East Chicago, Indiana could make it to the hills of Southern California, in one of its most beautiful cities? I can certainly tell you that I didn't dream of this not one day in my life before it happened. This wasn't always the case of having a beautiful home with a beautiful wife. I remember back in 2003 when I came off of my first deployment. My enlistment bonus kicked in while over there and I came back with over 10 grand to my name. That may not sound like a lot now, but to a 19 year old kid, it was the fortune of fortunes.

I purchased a car, a phone and finally ended up staying with a cousin of mines who was a retired Marine. I was thinking that I had it made. I had a roof over my head, my own whip and I was living in California. I thought the good times would last forever. Boy was I wrong. Over the next two years, I found myself spending recklessly. I went from 10g's to 8 g's, but I told myself that I was good. I dwindled down to 7 g's, yet still told myself that I was good. I told myself the same thing again once I got down to about 5 g's. Then, in 2005, right before I deployed for a second time in three years, I had less than 100 dollars to my name. I was down in the dumps. I had no money what so ever. Had it not been for me living on the ship, I wouldn't have had any money to make my monthly car payments. That's when I grew up. I said to myself that I would never be in this predicament again.

When I got back in November of that year, I started a plan. I would save and invest my money so that I would always be able and willing to pay my bills. In 2007, I moved into my first official crib in Oceanside, California. Trust me, it wasn't anything spectacular, but it was something that I could call my own. It was a modest one bedroom on top of a hill, but in a pretty rough part of the city.

The surroundings didn't faze me, seeing that I was from East Chicago and our hood looked way rougher. I decided to spend wisely in my new place. I started off by purchasing a let out couch from a mom and pops store for $125 dollars. It was inexpensive and provided me with something that I could lay my head down on. I felt like the King of England. It was just the beginning for me. As time went on, I added a TV, an additional couch, a box spring and mattress, dining room table and a few more items to make my place complete. It was a far cry from the lavish life, but to me it was the lavish life. I had set out to do what I wanted to do, all because I didn't repeat one process **(wasteful spending)**.

The new process that I did repeat (wise saving and spending) allowed me to have what I had. In 2009, I moved back to San Diego. Using the same plan I repeated, I moved into a two bedroom, two bathroom apartment near the beach. Now this was heaven for me. It was a long way from the one bedroom shack that I had. I had upgraded. I was happy and I was proud to call this place home. I stayed there for an additional three years until I took off to Guam. There, I moved into a one bedroom condo on the Pacific Ocean.

It was a major upgrade from living near the beach. I was literally right here on the ocean. I witnessed the greatest sunsets known to man. Every night, it was a warm 80 degrees. I would be amazed at how the Gecko's stuck to my window and ate the gnats who gathered around my window seal because of the living room lamp. I was truly living like a king on a tropical island, all because I repeated the plan that made me wise and not wasteful.

Flash forward to the current day. I come home everyday to a wife who genuinely cares and loves me for me. I have a home that others can only dream of. All this was the result of repeating a process that was beneficial and not ignorant. Just like the examples that I provided in my personal life, you must too become an example. Repeat the same thing you did to achieve a goal so that you can be on the way to achieve greatness!!!

STEP FIVE: SUCCESS

Here is the part of the book that most of you have been waiting on. This is the part that talks about success. What kind of success are we talking about? Well, there are many levels to success. See success doesn't just involve the first four steps.

No. Success involves a multitude of things including attitude, gain, loss, financial increase and a bunch of other variables. I will explain as I go along. When Michael Jordan took that last shot against the Utah Jazz, he not only went down in history with the greatest push off known to man, but he went down as one of the most successful men with his craft. I remember that shot like yesterday. He stripped Malone of the ball and dribbled down court. You already knew he was going to take the last shot. I was 13 years old and watching the game in my parents room. I can still hear Bob Costas voice with the call.

"Jordan...CHICAGO WITH THE LEAD!!!" I don't ever think anyone who was around at that time will ever forget that call. I know that for the longest after that, I would shoot in the gym and just leave my hand up after firing a jumper. I wanted to put myself in his shoes and just imagine what it would be like.

That success that he achieved that night was one of legacy. He cemented his legacy on the basketball court as arguably the greatest player to ever play the game of professional basketball (I still say Bill Russell). Not all of us will achieve that type of success however. We won't be remembered as a success for playing a sport. Maybe in a small town with high school lore someone will be remembered for that, but nine times out of ten, it won't happen. There are five different levels of success and I am about to discuss all of them so that you have a better understanding.

Level 1. Mental success.

– Know that you have accomplished much even when the journey to success throws a monkey wrench in your plans

Oh how I once again go back to the days of playing high school sports. When I played football for East Chicago Central, one of our biggest rivals on the field was Griffith High School. They were quarterbacked by Tyler Radtke and coached by his dad Russ Radtke. Oh how I and all of my teammates couldn't stand those guys. Especially Tyler!!! He had a mouth on him and he swore he was a God on the field.

It was my sophomore year of 2000. We were up 33–28 with less than a minute to go. The only way Griffith could win was by driving all the way down the field for a game winning score. No one at The Bone yard (an ode to their wishbone offense) thought it would be possible. In three plays however, he drove his team down 80 yards and scored the game winning touchdown. We ended up losing that game 35-33. The word hurt was an understatement. Our coaches made us feel like we were the true winners. It's called a moral victory. In my personal opinion, it is only good to give moral victories to kids who are very young. By the time we get to high school, all that moral victory crap is irrelevant. Then again, that is only in sports. Mental success can come in the form of just knowing that you completed a job or tasking.

I look at some of those shows on Food Network where they invite people to see if they can claim the title as top chef. In the end, there can only be one winner. What they fail to mention is that everyone who was invited on the show are already winners. Even for those who don't take home the title, they have already succeeded. This is called mental success. What they leave with is the thought process that they can achieve anything because they have already made it to the pinnacle. As an adult, we can't always win the top prize. That is not to say because you don't leave with the top prize that you are not a winner. The mental success you achieve from making it can lead to bigger success in the future.

Level 2. Financial success.
–Obtain wealth
–Distribute wealth
–Build up more wealth

So you work day and night to the bone sometimes just to put food on the table. We will just say you work in a steel mill. You risk getting burned on almost a daily basis. You are covered in filth from head to toe. You are just worn out by the end of each shift that you work. Unlike most of the workers around you, you have dreams of financial freedom. You don't want to labor for someone for the next thirty years. You don't want them to hand you a check, set your working hours or just plain rely on them for some medical benefits. No. You want financial freedom. You want to have the ability to create your own hours, your own cash flow and do as little as possible while earning the big bucks. I have numerous friends that are in the internet marketing business. They have seen great amounts of success with what they do. What's funny about it is that all the naysayers speak the same thing. "It's a pyramid scheme." I laugh at that, because let's go down, rather up the list of a normal corporation that everyday people work at.

-Workers

-Supervisors

-Managers

-Department heads or overseers

-Regional manager

-President

-Vice president

-Chief Operating Officer

-Chief Executive Officer

If your job is setup to something similar like this, chances are...YES!!! You do work in a pyramid scheme!!! That pyramid scheme is called an everyday 9 to 5. The world has been set up to think we have to work hard to make it. The 5% who don't work are the ones that control the 95%. While many continue on this path, there are those who don't want to feel the burden. They want the financial freedom that they well deserve.

The first step in achieving financial success is taking the risk. Many people are scared to play with money. What they don't realize is that money is nothing but a piece of paper. To make money you have to spend money. Those who have seen the most success financially have studied how to invest or sell good. It's the same thing that I am doing with my books and particularly this one. I am selling you a story on how to achieve greatness. Whether you buy into it is completely on you. If I wasn't me, and I had to meet me, I think I would take advice seeing that I literally went from almost rock bottom to where I am today. Money is not the root of all evil. The love of money is the root of all evil. Love is what you have the ability to do because of the money you earn. Getting up every day to the beat of your own drum is the greatest feeling in the world. We can all be there. We just have to get out of the mindsets of labor, labor and more labor that we are stuck in. True, there will always be someone who has to do a particular job. Just remember that there are 7 billion people on this earth. You do not have to be one of them.

Level 3. Naysayer success.
–Laugh at them
–Laugh even louder
–Continue doing you

This level of success is probably my favorite one of them all. It is the one directed towards the haters. Now, let's make this clear. Everyone doesn't have haters. That term is too loosely thrown around. To have haters, you have to be doing something extra ordinary that others want to do, but simply can't. Now,

I'm just going to run down a few of the things naysayers told me wasn't possible.

"You aren't going to write any books."–This is book number 5. All previous books have sold on all six habitable continents.

"You aren't going to make it in spoken word."–Has performed with Def Poets such as Ise Lyfe and Black Ice. Opened for Joe, Jon B. and Dwele (All Grammy nominated artists).

"You aren't going to make it back to the football field."–Made it back to the football field in 2007 to play for the Marines after tearing my ACL/PCL/MCL and lateral meniscus the previous year. Made All Marine selection for Camp Pendleton at DL/LB.

I won't go into anymore accolades of mine as I will just leave these right here for you all to see. Naysayer success is the sweetest because it is the one that shuts everyone who told you that you couldn't do it up. Oh how they hate to see you come out on top when all they did was doubt you. What is even better about naysayer success is how you react to it.

The proper reaction to naysayer success is to not even talk about it. Think about it. Naysayers pride themselves off of running their mouths, telling everyone and their momma about your dreams. Notice I said your dreams and not theirs. They usually don't have any. They have no aspirations in life. They just want to move with the motions of the earth. Sorry to say, but they remind you of the house niggers in the slave days. The just wanted to follow master around and talk about all the slaves that were out in the fields.

Naysayers feed off of negative energy. So when you become successful, do not feed them negative energy back by talking mess about them. I used to be that way. I used to pride myself off proving people wrong. Then, I would rub it in their face with obscene words and gestures. I thought that's what I had to do, until I realized that it did more bad than good. All it did was fuel the naysayers even more to run their mouth. They would always come with the

"Well you can't do this" speech. Then, I

would find myself out trying to prove to them again that I could do whatever it was that they said I couldn't. As I got older, I realized one thing. You do not have to prove anything to anyone in this lifetime except God and yourself. See most of the time, naysayers get upset because you aren't doing things the way they want it to be done. This is either caused by two things.

One, they just feel that their way is better than everyone else's.

Two, their way is laziness, and they don't want to see anyone reach success. When you do however reach success, your reaction should be one of a simple smile and a continue on about your day attitude. Don't say anything. That makes naysayers even madder. They have nothing to combat with. They have no one entertaining them. That makes them irrelevant more than what they already are. It fuels their fire. Once they see that they can't affect you anymore, they move on to someone else, saying the same thing. The cycle never stops for them. Never and I mean never let those clowns bring you down as a person. That is their job. Make those haters unemployed when it comes to you. Know that you will rise above negativity.

LEVEL 4. Death success.

–Old ways must die

–You have to be willing to accept new ways of operating

–Do not reach back in your past

Now I know for a fact that may just read the line next to level four and popped their eyes open. What in the good hell is Death success? Well why you are asking me, take the time to close the book for a minute and think about what comes to mind when you hear it. I'll be waiting for you as soon as you open it back up.

Okay. You're back? Good. They say that when a baby is born into this world, someone else dies. To give life one has to lose life. The same can be associated when it comes to success. I learned over time that when you want to enhance one area of your life, you have to bring death to another area of your life. The only way that you will reach a successful plateau in anything that you do is to bring death to some of your worldly ways. Take the CEO of Uprock Publications, the company who puts out my books. Now, I am about to explain some of his life story. Don't worry, it won't cause backlash between us because he has already put his life story out there for all to see.

Mr. Caujuan Mayo took a chance on me when I was unsure of a lot in the author world. His story is unique. He is an ex-felon who went to the big house due to his involvement in the pimp game. Now, upon his release from prison, he turned that negative into something positive. That came in the form of writing books. Now with his own publication company, he has given authors like me a chance to express themselves on a worldwide platform. See in order for him to have established this company, he had to put one of his old ways of living to rest. He had to let it die. It's the same way with all of us. I remember how before I got married, I would want to still head out to a nightspot and maybe flirt with a few of the ladies just for old time's sake. It would be nothing serious, but I was just having fun. Now, as a married man, I have stopped all that. There is no more flirting with the females. I don't want one to mistake it for being something serious and all of a sudden I have another problem on my hand.

To have a successful marriage, me and my wife had to put death to a lot of things in our lives. When I find myself upset and ready to go ham in some situations, I have to put old ways of handling business to rest before thinking about another way on how to resolve a conflict. I put death to the ignat acting guy a long time ago, as I realized there was better ways of handling stuff. Death in success, much like death in the physical form, is actually not death. It is simply a form of new life. When someone dies, we speak their life as continuing in a heavenly realm. So in actuality, they never die. They just exist in an entirely different universe. With success, your ways that you have brought death to truly never go away. They are always inside of you. You have just simply harnessed a way to dwell new life within you to master your craft. When I brought death to baggy clothes, I brought life to a more grown up dress game. When I brought death to my worldly ways, I brought more life to the spiritual side that dwells inside of me. When I brought death to old relationships and old ways, I gave life to a relationship that has more than prospered and benefited me. Death is truly the beginning.

LEVEL 5. Celebrity success.
–Be ready for bright lights
–Be ready for dull nights
–Embrace and persevere

You have seen the vision and you have watched it manifest into something that even you couldn't imagine. Countless days of planning and preparing helped you get to this level. Long, tiresome nights seemed like they weren't worth it, but now you see the benefits of your hard work and dedication to your dream. You have done it and it is something that no one can take away from you.

Congratulations, you have now reached a level of success only seen by a very few. Celebrity success is crazy because at some point in our lives, we all dream about being that star athlete or actor walking down the red carpet. We imagine getting stopped by photographers and having our pictures taken with every single move. Celebrity status has you on the map and known by everyone known to man. Even if you don't have the international spotlight, there is still the national spotlight or even the regional spotlight.

What many people don't realize is that everyone that ended up with eyes on them nationally came from humble beginnings. Many great actors started off in simple theatre plays hoping to get recognized. A great singer or comedian frequented the open mic scenes in their city or region for years before getting noticed. On rare occasions, some people become overnight celebrities. Most of the time that is simply not the case. It takes months, maybe years to achieve that level of stardom. Once you get it, the real work has just begun. Let's take a look at both sides, starting with myself.

I remember once traveling to Oakland with one of my ex girlfriends. She was from the Bay Area and it was my first time up there. Honestly, Oakland isn't necessarily on anyone's gem list, as the city is a rough and rugged one. It actually looks a lot like Gary, Indiana with hills. So we were walking through downtown headed to a theatre to see my main man Ise Lyfe "Pistols & Prayers" theatre piece. As we get up to the building, the woman outside of the building says

"I know you." Inside, I froze up. I know I hadn't cheated on my girlfriend, so my next question I was wondering was where I know her from. Soon after she said

"You're that poet from San Diego." Inside I let out a sigh of relief. God indeed was real.

That was shocking to me because as I said earlier, that was my first time to Oakland. What that had shown me was that my celebrity had went far beyond a lowly part of San Diego. Later I would experience the same thing before traveling to Guam from a woman who was from the island. I was known over there before I had even stepped foot over there. That indeed was a feeling that to this day I still can't explain.

This is the good part of celebrity success. When people can look at you and clamor just from being in your presence. It's knowing that you are making people feel good from the things that you are doing. Or, it's simply the fact that people want to see you just so they can brag to their friends that they seen you. Trust me, I am not on the celebrity tip like Brad Pitt. I don't have fans following me everywhere I go or trying to take pictures of me while I am eating in a restaurant. It does however feel good to be known on sight by people outside of your state. Now, let us look at the negative side of celebrity. Look at what I just said about Brad Pitt. Fans are trying to take pictures of you wherever you go. That is the first downside of celebrity success. You really don't have a private life anymore. The things that you were able to do as a normal human being are nonexistent anymore. If you go to a restaurant, people will either snap pictures of you or they may interrupt your meal and actually try to seek an autograph while you are eating.

That is so disrespectful, but not all people have common decency. It is something that just comes with the territory. Years ago Halle Berry had to take a paparazzi group to court for snapping pictures of her and her kid. This one I definitely agreed with. Leave kids out of it. They didn't ask for all the glitz and glamour. As a person who loves children as well, they need to be protected. We already have enough sick nuts in this world who are child molesters. No one knows if that camera is snapping a picture for the National Enquirer or some sick nut that wants to kidnap a child and do bodily harm to them. It is not cool and

I pray that if I reach a level like that one day, my kids won't have to suffer through it. Another downfall of the celebrity success is that the world looks at you as being mistake free. No longer are you human in their eyes. You are above the human being status quo. Many people get DUI's on a regular. The minute you as the celebrity get one, all of a sudden your whole life story is broadcast on CNN.

Paul Walker, the beloved actor from the Fast and Furious movie series died in a horrific car crash. What followed was a bunch of public idiots shaming his death because of speeding. Well I want to know what human on Earth goes the speed limit ever. Don't worry...I'll wait. My point is this. With celebrity comes public opinion that is most of the time just plain stupid. People will hit you with the

"You're not better than us because you have money." Celebrities 99.9% of the time never say they're better than the average Joe. A lot of people just assume they are self centered because they have made it. With celebrity success, you have to learn that it is vital to tune out public opinion. Another negative about being a celeb besides privacy and public opinion is that you are what you are. A CELEB!!! You all of a sudden become bigger than The Pope. Ok, maybe you won't become that large, but you do get what I am saying.

In the world we live in, people pay attention more to celebrity news than they do things that will affect their everyday lifestyles. People know more about the relationship of two celebrities than the budget cuts to inner city schools. They will report all day over the dresses three actresses wore instead of being focused on why there are little girls across America who don't have any clothes to put on their backs.

That is the bad thing about being a celebrity. It gives the world a false vision. This is the primary reason people blame celebrities for the problems that go on in the world. As a black man, I have heard so many people say that Michael Jordan is a coon because they purchased all of his shoes and he hasn't given back. Well first off, they are all wrong because Michael Jordan does give back through numerous charities. Two, no one told their dumb tails to keep purchasing shoes that have been out since before I was a teen. As a celebrity, especially a black celebrity, people are going to expect you to save their situation. It is something that you cannot avoid. I'm going to just keep it 100 right here and maybe make some people mad.

The real truth as to why some communities are in disarray isn't because of the celebrities. It is simply because the residents of the community are lazy. I'm black so I will speak on what I know. I grew up seeing many peers of mine who were worse off than me come to school fresh to death. When you looked around the same neighborhood where they were from, it looked like a war zone. Now imagine if parents stopped spending $200 dollars on shoes and just donated $20 a paycheck to support the whole community. Let's say a block in the hood has 30 houses on it. Out of those 30 households, 15 have both parents. Five are single parent homes. And let's just make the other 10 homes on the block apartment buildings. They have a total of 10 families in each, making for 20 parents.

Now, let's do the math. The 15 homes with both parents can pull $40 form both mother and father. 15 multiplied by $40 is $600. Out of the five single parent homes, you will obtain $100. Now, the 200 remaining tenants in the apartment building $20 donation will equate to $4000. That adds up to a grand total of $4700. Instead of buying shoes for all the kids in the neighborhood, that money could be used towards community food, school supplies, nice clothes for all the kids to have, games or books. With that kind of money, the community can even come together to supply a trip for the children of the community to go to a natural history museum, or some form of educational trip.

As a whole, we have to do better in the communities that we are living in. Sure, being a celebrity means your voice will be taken a little bit more serious. However, do not take on the full load. A loud mouth soldier is only as effective as the group who is behind him.

BONUS: THE MOTIVATION

As I close out this book and read back over the words I wrote, I realize even more that what I just did was not for me. It was truly for someone else. Yes I can go further in life, but right now, it is time to teach, enhance and allow the new generation to thrive.

When I created a five step process towards achieving greatness, I did it with the intention to make someone achieve it on all levels. It wasn't just for writing or speaking. It was for anything that you set your mind to. If you want to dig out caves all of your life, then by all means be the greatest cave digger that ever walked the face of the earth. Where it all starts is within us as people. We have to listen to that positive inner voice that tells us to go out and be great. We have to be willing to look in the mirror and say I will do it. I will make it. Nothing or no one will stop me from achieving my goals.

The biggest obstacle is and has always been us as the individual. Motivation doesn't have to come from myself or any book. Motivation comes from within. My entire life, I have been motivating myself to be the best damn Joe McClain Jr. that I could be. I am the type of person who walks around with a chip on their shoulder when it comes to everything. That is how I maintain a level of high standards when it comes to anything I am doing.

I pretend like the world is against me. If I fail, the world will come crashing down. With that mindset, I have been able to achieve some pretty great things in my life. I remember August 9, 2015 like it was yesterday. My beautiful wife set me up to meet one of my idols. CT Fletcher. As I got out of the car and seen him, he said

"You hear to get your ass kicked today."
It was the most grueling workout of my then
30 year life. My whole motivation during that
ass whooping session was seeing that I was
with the legend himself and that there would
be no way in hell that I would quit. By the end
of our workout, honest to God truth, I couldn't
even lift my arms up. I couldn't even do one
push up. I left it all in the Iron Addicts Gym in
Long Beach.

When I got to the ship the next day to being
sea trials, I wasn't able to work out. I managed
to work out the second day out to sea, but
even that was a struggle. I didn't fully recover
for a week. That was indeed however the best
damn recovery that I could ever imagine. He
motivated me to the core, but I motivated
myself even more.

Mentally, you have to break the chains as he
says. Everything starts with that thing that sits
on our necks. Our brains. You don't have to be
the smartest to lead. You just have to have the
gift of bringing people together for one

common purpose. I have done that on so many occasions. Trust me, I am not the brightest bulb in the room. There are many who are smarter and more gifted than I am. That is okay. Everyone isn't meant to have the same gifts. Each person unique qualities are to be brought together to form one common goal. That goal is success.

As I spoke throughout this book on numerous topics, one thing I never said is can't. You need to X that word out of your vocabulary if it is in there. Saying you can't automatically will have you losing the battle. Saying you can't downgrades you as a human. The words I can't shouldn't even be in the English language if you ask me.

The only time you should say you can't is when you can't say it. That will be when you are lying in a casket for your final ride. I was almost at that final ride multiple times in my life. From the times my heart would act up to the dangerous situations I escaped in East Chicago and San Diego, I escaped death. Once you face death, then can you have a true appreciation of life. My wife is no stranger to death either. She survived two strokes as a youth. She is my motivation because when I get weak, she instantly becomes my strength. Her fight was more grueling than mine. I dealt with heart issues since the age of 12, but I didn't have major problems until the age of 16. She had to relearn how to write, think, speak, spell, all of that going into her teenage years. Now, she is a beautiful woman with a beautiful heart who has beautifully brought major increase to my life. As I end this motivation for you all, I have one last thing to say. This book is dedicated to my loving wife for all of eternity, CHAZ MARIE CUNNINGHAM-MCCLAIN. I love you dearly sweetheart.

ABOUT THE AUTHOR

It's amazing what can happen when pen meets a paper. The ideas that are brought forth by the author can turn a simple thought into a masterpiece. How did Joe McClain get into writing??? That's a great question to ask. Living in Guam back in 2013, he took interest in a short story contest that was originated by Brianni Blue, a well known spoken word artist out of Oakland, CA, who appeared on TV One's

"Versus and Flow." Poetry was always easy, but to write a full length story??? That was a different ball game and one Joe had no idea how to comprehend.

"My biggest thing was simply what to write about. I would literally sit in front of my computer for an hour and not type anything," he says. After much debate, he turned on some old Dipset and the rest was history.

"JR Writer was spitting a verse on one track, and immediately I came up with the title of THE WRITERS BLOCK. From there, I began to write about my life and add some thrill to my story for entertainment purposes."

In a span of 30 days, Joe had finished his first story, and added another notch to his resume. Fast Forward to February 2014. He had now returned stateside to California. During a visit to the Lyrical Exchange open mic in San Diego, a longtime friend, DJ Redlite, put him in contact with Caujuan Mayo, a friend of his who also ran his own publishing company.

"I wasn't even thinking about getting the story published. I honestly did it to pass the time by while I was living over there, and because I thought it would be something cool to do." After contacting Caujuan and arranging a meeting with him, the two immediately hit it off and began to talk business.

Two weeks later, after careful analysis of this new situation, Joe signed on the dotted line for "THE WRITERS BLOCK" to be published. On August 4th, 2014, "THE WRITERS BLOCK" was released and took off to be a hit in the short story genre.

"I honestly didn't know what to expect. When I seen and read the reviews people were leaving me on Amazon, I know I had indeed did something special." To this date, "THE WRITERS BLOCK" has sold over 1,000 copies and continues to sell. With this project under his belt, Joe released his second book entitled "BANDAGES" in March of 2015.

"It's a well thought out story," he says.

"This isn't Writer's Block. With that book, I put together something and didn't think to much of it. After seeing how well people received it, I really studied the process of writing and putting collective thoughts into a great story that people could really relate to. If I'm not upgrading, then I'm downgrading."

How this young man transitioned into an unknown arena and made it work for him is beyond amazing. As a product of the inner city, he is really transcending the art of writing by opening people up to a world that many have not experienced.

Television can only give you a glimpse. To make a person feel like they are actually there, that is something completely different. Joe McClain Jr. is definitely on the way to becoming a top tier author and more importantly, an excellent figure in the black community who shows that anything is indeed possible. He has many more book projects planned to include "The Square Rt of Pain" and "BANDAGES 2: Wounds Re-opened." What is forthcoming for this great author is beyond amazing. If the world does not know who he is, they will certainly know very soon.

IF YOU ENJOYED READING
"P.E.E.R.S"
PLEASE LEAVE A REVIEW ON AMAZON.COM
http://ow.ly/JggvZ

We Keep The "P" In Publications

20 UPROCK 12

·PUBLICATIONS·

Website: www.uprockpublications.com
Emails: uprockp@gmail.com
Facebook: uprockpublications
Twitter: uprockpub
Contact: (619) 259-0298